The well-known story of how God helped Noah to keep his family and the creatures on Earth safe from the flood is retold for young children. It is based on the Book of Genesis, Chapters 6, 7, 8 and 9.

British Library Cataloguing in Publication Data
Murdock, Hy
   Noah's Ark. — (Ladybird Bible stories)
   1. Noah's ark — Juvenile literature
   2. Bible stories. English — O.T. Genesis
   I. Title   II. Grundy, Lynn N.
   222'.1109505   BS580.N6
   ISBN 0-7214-9517-6

First Edition

Published by Ladybird Books Ltd Loughborough Leicestershire UK
Ladybird Books Inc Lewiston Maine 04240 USA
© LADYBIRD BOOKS LTD MCMLXXXV
© Illustrations LYNN N GRUNDY MCMLXXXV

Noah's Ark

written by HY MURDOCK
illustrated by LYNN N GRUNDY

Ladybird Books

There was once a time when God was very angry with the people of the world. He could see that they were selfish and unkind to each other. He saw them do many bad things.

God decided to punish everyone by sending rain to make a great flood.

But there was one man called Noah
who had made God happy. He was a
good man. God wanted Noah to be safe
when the flood came so He told him to
make a special boat called an ark.

God told Noah how to make the ark. It was to be built using gopher wood; it had to have many rooms; it had to be waterproof inside and outside; and it had to be 300 cubits long, 50 cubits wide and 30 cubits high.

(A cubit was as long as a grown-up's arm, from the elbow to the end of the middle finger.)

The ark had to have a window and also
a door at the side.

God told Noah to take his family with him and also to take males and females of all the creatures on the earth.

Noah needed to take enough food for the people and all the animals. He had to work very hard because the rain would begin soon.

When the ark was ready, Noah and his family went inside. Then all the animals went through the door, two at a time.

The rain came. It rained and rained and rained. The flood rose higher and higher. God made it rain for forty days and forty nights.

There was so much rain that the water covered all the earth and even some of the high mountains.

At last the rain stopped. After a long time Noah opened the window and sent a bird called a raven to look for any land. The raven flew backwards and forwards but all he could find was water. Next Noah sent a dove but the dove came back to the ark.

After seven days Noah sent the dove
again to see if there was land.

Before dark, the dove came back with
the leaf from an olive tree in her beak.
She had found land. Now Noah knew
that the flood would soon go.

After another seven days Noah sent the dove again. This time the bird did not come back so Noah knew that the earth would soon be dry.

Then God told Noah that it was time to leave the ark. Noah, his family and all the animals came out of the ark and began a new life on the earth.

Noah said thank you to God for keeping them safe. God made a rainbow in the sky and promised that He would never send another flood which would cover the whole earth.